Date: 6/29/18

J 971 MAR
Markovics, Adam,
Canada /

Countries We Come From

Canada

by Adam Markovics

Consultant: Karla Ruiz
Teacher's College, Columbia University
New York, New York

BEARPORT PUBLISHING

New York, New York

Credits

Cover, © Africa Studio/Shutterstock and Songquan Deng/iStock; 3, © Dan Breckwoldt/Shutterstock; 4, © Alberto Loyo/Shutterstock; 5T, © Eduard Kyslynskyy/Shutterstock; 5B, © DebraH/Shutterstock; 7, © All Canada Photos/Alamy; 8, © Dennis W. Donohue/Shutterstock; 8–9, © Harry Beugelink/Shutterstock; 9T, © Pim Leijen/Shutterstock; 9B, © Holly Kuchera/Shutterstock; 10–11, © Galyna Andrushko/Dreamstime; 11, © Eric Baccega/AGE fotostock; 12T, © Sabena Jane Blackbird/Alamy; 12B, © North Wind Picture Archives/Alamy; 13, © North Wind Picture Archives/Alamy; 15, © Vlad G/Shutterstock; 16–17, © SurangaSL/Shutterstock; 17, © Richard Cavalleri/Shutterstock; 18, © Sergei Bachlakov/Shutterstock; 19, © Design Pics Inc/Alamy; 20, © Phil McDonald/Shutterstock; 21, © Rubens Abboud/Alamy; 22T, © Sian Cox/Dreamstime; 22B, © Kim D. Lyman/Shutterstock; 23, © Magdalena Kucova/Shutterstock; 24–25, © Cal Sport Media/Alamy; 25, © mexrix/Shutterstock; 26, © krausphoto/iStock; 27, © LSOphoto/iStock; 28L, © AF archive/Alamy; 28R, © Olga Popova/Shutterstock; 29, © SFM Press Reporter/Alamy; 30T, © Africa Studio/Shutterstock and © Fat Jackey/Shutterstock; 30B, © Joshua Resnick/Shutterstock; 31 (T to B), © Vlad G/Shutterstock, © Galyna Andrushko/Dreamstime, © Pink Candy/Shutterstock, © Marc Bruxelle/Shutterstock, and © Alberto Loyo/Shutterstock; 32, © neftali/Shutterstock.

Publisher: Kenn Goin
Senior Editor: Joyce Tavolacci
Creative Director: Spencer Brinker
Design: Debrah Kaiser
Photo Researcher: Thomas Persano

Library of Congress Cataloging-in-Publication Data

Names: Markovics, Adam, author.
Title: Canada / by Adam Markovics.
Description: New York, New York : Bearport Publishing, [2017] | Series: Countries we come from | Includes bibliographical references and index. | Audience: Ages 6–10.
Identifiers: LCCN 2016015161 (print) | LCCN 2016015408 (ebook) | ISBN 9781944998271 (library binding) | ISBN 9781944998288 (ebook)
Subjects: LCSH: Canada—Juvenile literature.
Classification: LCC F1008.2 .M296 2017 (print) | LCC F1008.2 (ebook) | DDC 971—dc23
LC record available at https://lccn.loc.gov/2016015161

For more information, write to Bearport Publishing Company, Inc., 45 West 21st Street, Suite 3B, New York, New York 10010. Printed in the United States of America.

10 9 8 7 6 5 4 3 2 1

Contents

This Is Canada

HUGE

WILD

Friendly

Canada is **vast**.

It covers a large part of North America.

It's the second-largest country in the world!

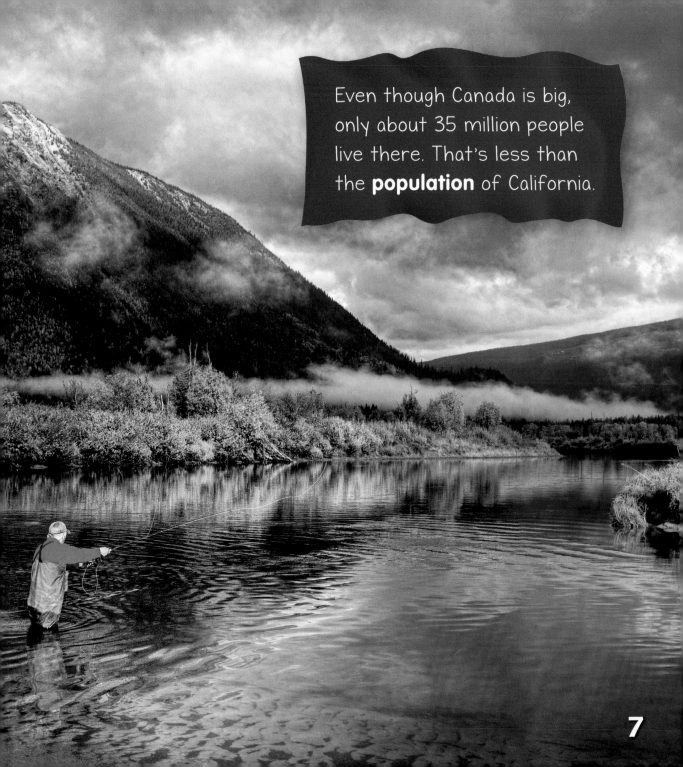

Even though Canada is big, only about 35 million people live there. That's less than the **population** of California.

More than half of Canada is covered with forests.

The forests are home to bears, caribou, and wolves.

grizzly bear

caribou

gray wolf

Canada has thousands of lakes.

9

The far north of Canada is cold and icy.

Few trees grow there.

Glaciers stretch across the frozen land.

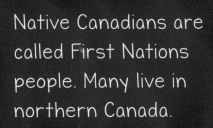

Native Canadians are called First Nations people. Many live in northern Canada.

glacier

People first came to Canada about 30,000 years ago.

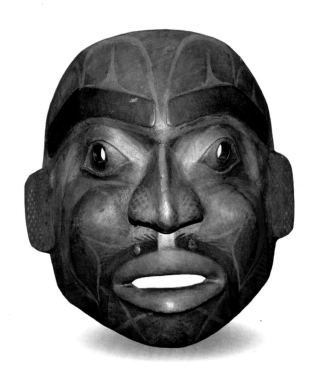

In the 1600s, the French and British arrived.

They fought to rule Canada.

In 1763, the British took control of the country.

In 1931, Canada became a free country.

13

Canada is made up of
10 provinces and 3 territories.

Provinces and territories are
similar to states.

The **capital** of Canada is Ottawa. It's located in the province of Ontario.

Most Canadians live in cities.

Toronto is the biggest.

Its tall buildings soar into the sky.

The second-largest city in Canada is Montreal.

Many Canadians speak English and French.

This is how you say *hi* in French:

Salut (sah-LOO)

This is how you say *snow*:

La Neige (LA NEJ)

Most people in the province of Quebec speak French.

There are special police in Canada.
They're called Mounties.

Many Mounties get around on horses.

Mounties are known for their red uniforms.

Canada is famous for maple syrup.
The syrup is made from tree **sap**!

First, people
collect the sap.

Then they boil
it until it's sweet
and sticky!

People enjoy maple syrup on pancakes and waffles.

23

In Canada, people love ice hockey.

Two teams skate on a rink.

The players try to whack a puck into the other team's net. Goal!

hockey puck

Hockey is the most popular sport in Canada.

Canadians also like to enjoy the outdoors.

In winter, they ski and snowboard.

In summer, they hike.

Canadians also enjoy swimming in the country's many lakes.

Some of the funniest people in the world are Canadian.

Jim Carrey

Just think of Jim Carrey and Martin Short!

Martin Short

Canadian Lorne Michaels created *Saturday Night Live*. It's the best-known comedy show on TV.

Fast Facts

Capital city: Ottawa

Population of Canada: More than 35 million

Main languages: English and French

Money: Canadian dollar

Major religions: Christianity and Islam

Neighboring country: United States

Cool Fact: Canadians eat more macaroni and cheese than people from any other country in the world!

capital (KAP-uh-tuhl) a city where a country's government is based

glaciers (GLAY-shurz) huge, slow-moving rivers of snow and ice

population (pop-yuh-LAY-shuhn) the total number of people living in a place

sap (SAP) a liquid that flows through trees and carries food and nutrients

vast (VAST) huge in size

31

Index

Read More

Landau, Elaine. *Canada (True Books: Countries).* New York: Children's Press (2000).

McDonnell, Ginger. *Next Stop: Canada (Time for Kids).* Huntington Beach, CA: Teacher Created Materials (2011).

Learn More Online

To learn more about Canada, visit
www.bearportpublishing.com/CountriesWeComeFrom

About the Author

Adam Markovics was born in Montreal, Canada, and now lives in Ossining, New York. He thinks Canadians are hilarious.